Mackinaw Loves Its Bridge

Memories of the Construction of the Mackinac Bridge

by
Mary Lou Peters

Mary Lou Peters

D1490242

Mackinaw Area Historical Society
P. O. Box 999,
Mackinaw City, MI 49701

From Fritz & Marion Phelps

ISBN 0-9795133-0-8

Printed in Canada

Front cover photo: Ken Teysen
Back cover photo: Sandy Planisek

Mackinaw Area Historical Society
P. O. Box 999
Mackinaw City, MI 49701

This book is dedicated to the residents of Mackinaw City
   —those who have lived here all their lives as well as those who are relative newcomers
   —and the way they all work together to make this village a very special place to live.

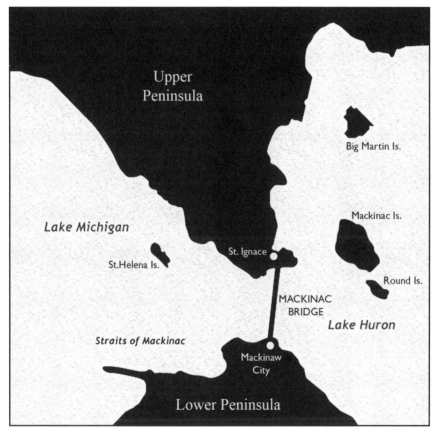

The Straits of Mackinac now spanned by the Mackinac Bridge

INTRODUCTION

As a relative newcomer to Mackinaw City, I still consider the Mackinac Bridge a novelty. I never tire of seeing the first glimpse of it as I round the bend on my daily walking route along Huron Avenue. As I get to know the people who make this town such a special place, I hear fascinating and entertaining stories of the bridge and how it has impacted life in this small northern community. Because there is no manufacturing here, Mackinaw City residents have to be resourceful. They find a niche and make a living. The bridge changed the way residents worked and played, and caused many lives to take different directions.

Aside from practical matters, the Mackinac Bridge is a connection between generations. Many of the people interviewed for this book have lived here all their lives. Some of them are second-generation residents who raised their families here and are now watching their great-grandchildren grow up nearby. Some are still running the same family businesses their parents started when they first came to this area. All of them have a strong attachment to the bridge. Because of their reverent attitudes toward the bridge, I have come to look at it with the same awe and wonder. Through the process of collecting these small-town stories, I've come to realize what a special place this is. I'm proud to call Mackinaw City my adoptive hometown.

Mary Lou Peters

THE BRIDGE CONSTRUCTION BROUGHT NEW FRIENDS AND SOME TROUBLEMAKERS

Long before the bridge was built, around 1942, sixteen-year-old Don Darrow hauled stone in his father's dump truck from Gulliver, near Manistique in the Upper Peninsula, to St. Ignace, a one-way trip of ninety miles. "If you go out on that side of the bridge (west of the ticket office on the St. Ignace end), you'll see all that stone and stuff we put in there," said Don. "They had an idea back then that there was going to be something there, a bridge of some kind. That approach was put there for that reason." Then came WWII and bridge planning came to a halt.

Don and Theresa Darrow

During the bridge construction years, Don and Theresa Darrow bought their little cottage on Wenniway Drive, on the Straits of Mackinac, where they watched the bridge being built from their front windows. They were busy with many things at that time, raising two children and Don's work for the Mackinaw City Police Department.

1

As a policeman, Don watched drifters come into town looking for one of the thousands of bridge construction jobs that were rumored to be had. These transients had placed all their hope in getting a bridge job. "They were broke," Don remembered. "There used to be a lot of tents in the campground near where the fort is now, at Carp Lake, and south of Mackinaw."

Some of those who were fortunate enough to get a job building the bridge gave the local police department some trying times. It was quite common for Don and his fellow police officers to have to break up bar fights between the workers from different trades. "Those guys would come in at night (to McLellan's Bar where Shepler's dock is now located) to have their drinks," Don said. "The electricians would fight against the ironworkers. Every outfit would get into a scrap with another one and I'd have to take them down to jail."

But Theresa remembers that not all bridge workers were troublesome. The Darrows developed a long-lasting friendship with Vern and Ginny Luft, superintendent of the road crew and his wife. "They used to live in one of the houses on the shore," she said. "We used to go over to their house and they'd come over to our house." Theresa took care of their kids occasionally. Even after the Lufts packed up and moved on to the next job, they kept in contact and returned to Mackinaw once in a while to see their friends and the bridge.

Don recalled that the bridge's grand opening brought more people to Mackinaw City than its four-man police department could handle. "They had the National Guard up here, about a hundred of them, and they brought up the motorcycle cops from Detroit," he said.

In 1957, just after the bridge opened up, Don's parents started a little drive-in restaurant in their garage next to the seven-bedroom house where Don had grown up with his six brothers and two sisters. The site, once a farm way outside of town, is just a block away from the bridge's southern approach. In fact, you can still find a little cement silo base near the restaurant's parking lot. The bridge brought a lot more tourists to town—people coming through Mackinaw City to go to the Upper Peninsula or just to look at the bridge—so there was a need for a restaurant to accommodate all these visitors.

Theresa remembers the simple menu the Darrows began with. "We served hamburgers, hot dogs, onion rings, French fries, and root beer in frosted mugs," she said. "Pretty soon we needed more room so we tore the house down and we built on. We had outside bathrooms. Then all of a sudden they (the customers) wanted soup, chili, mashed potatoes, and first thing you know we just started a full-sized restaurant." The restaurant is now famous for its homemade pies.

Borrow pit

Central Ave. passing
under bridge's on-ramp

Railroad track coming into town

M.J. Duggan, Michigan Dept. of Transportation, Mackinac Bridge Authority

*Bridge dedication day in 1958. This photo looks southwest. Cars are parked
everywhere, including along both sides of I-75. You can also see the "borrow pit" from
which dirt was scraped to build the ramp up to the bridge.*

The pies all started with Mrs. Parker, a dedicated employee who took great pride in her work. Theresa remembers Mrs. Parker's first efforts: "She'd make apple, cherry, and just a few kinds of pie. Back then we used all our own homemade fillings, and I still do that." Now the pie list at Darrow's Family Restaurant is the main part of the menu board that greets customers as they walk through the door. "When we're really busy we're up to 60, 65 pies a day," she said. Customers are disappointed when the restaurant runs out of their favorite pie, but Theresa recalls advice she got from a long-time restaurant owner: "It's better to run out than throw out."

In October, when Darrow's Restaurant closes for the winter, townspeople begin counting down the days until their re-opening in May. Since 1988 Don and Theresa's son Randy and his wife, Traci, have been in partnership at the restaurant, continuing the family tradition. Don and Theresa are enjoying retirement in their lakefront home on the site of the small cottage they lived in so many years ago. Their wide front windows give an exquisite panorama of the Straits of Mackinac. "What a view!" Don exclaimed.

"It's beautiful," agreed Theresa. "Sometimes, in the summertime when the water is calm, it's just like a mirror and it reflects the bridge and all the lights. It's really great."

And, as if one view of the bridge isn't enough, the Darrows have two. A wall-size mirror in their living room gives them a picture perfect sight from either of their recliners. A favorite pastime of theirs is watching ship traffic on the Straits. During our visit Don picked up the *Know Your Ships* book and identified the Stewart J. Cort as it glided under the bridge.

Don recalled, "Everybody thought that when the bridge was built the town was done, but it wasn't. So many people coming up here to see the bridge, so many people going across the bridge, the town didn't die. It's just been a pretty good thing for the town."

Don's family home where Darrow's Restaurant is now

4

THE BRIDGE WAS GOOD FOR BUSINESS

Emma and Lester Stokes are both in their nineties and they have experienced a lot of Mackinaw City's history firsthand. The house they live in, just a few blocks from the Mackinac Bridge, has been their home for 69 years. Before that it was Emma's grandparents' home. Emma's parents' home was purchased by the State of Michigan and moved to make room for the approach to the bridge.

Like several other Mackinaw City residents, Emma's father was a skeptic regarding the bridge. Emma explained: "My dad would say, 'They'll never build a bridge. They'll never do it.'" Her mother always wished he'd lived long enough to see the bridge go up but Emma offers another view. "I think it would have been very difficult for him to see them come along and say they were going to take his home."

 The State of Michigan didn't offer them a choice about selling their home though, and Lester says they didn't give Emma's mother much money for her

Emma (Sands) and Lester Stokes

house and three lots. "Just barely enough to buy another place to move into," he said.

The Stokes tell about the fun times they had while the bridge was being built. Lester's friend, Harry Hadinger, owned a two-seat airplane that he taught Lester to fly. "We each had a camera," Lester recalled. "We'd take a ride while they were working on the bridge and I'd snap my pictures. He'd go over on one side and back on the other. Then I'd take over and take the same route, and he'd take his pictures."

By 1956 some of the south end of the bridge was finished, so Lester and Emma, along with other townspeople, would occasionally drive out onto the wooden ramp at the work site to take a look at the construction progress. But, because it wasn't officially allowed, they had to be careful to avoid getting caught. "We drove out on there on the weekends when they weren't working," Emma said. "It was fun driving out that far."

The bridge piers were in place and the framework for the deck was being strung across the piers when this aerial photo was taken.

Lester's work on the car ferries took him past the bridge where he and his co-workers would make their observations. "Every day you could see something new," he said.

But the completion of the bridge would mean that the car ferries would no longer be needed to transport people and vehicles between the upper and lower peninsulas. "The day the bridge was finished I was out of a job," Lester said. "I'd been there about 15 years. They (the State of Michigan) offered me a job over on the other side of the bridge to drive truck or snowplow, but I'd have to move over there. I said, 'I live right at the foot of the bridge. Why should I move to St. Ignace?' They said, 'Well, we can't take you if you don't live in St. Ignace.' So I was out of a job."

Faced with a family to support, Lester purchased a local Texaco gas station. "It was right where Alice's candy store (Alice's Kandy and Korn on S. Huron Ave.) is right now," he said. "The gas pumps were out in the street, outside the sidewalk." After three successful years there, Lester expanded by managing a new service station on the other end of town at 200 S. Nicolet, on the site of the old railroad bunkhouse. Since then it has been a restaurant and now it is a retail clothing shop.

The bridge was good for business. Lester ran his two stations successfully for 20 years. "At the time the bridge was built, Soapy (G. Mennen Williams) was governor," said Lester. "When he was here in town, he used to stay at my folks' cabins (on N. Nicolet, east of the approach). They'd have conventions on the island (Mackinac Island) and lots of times they'd leave their car with us at our gas station. I had a sign out there to do that kind of service. I'd go down to the boat with them, let them unload, and I'd bring their car back. We'd give them a claim check. When the convention was coming off the island, they'd call us and tell us what boat they'd be arriving on and we'd bring their cars to meet them at the boat. They thought that was a good service. I wasn't the only one. There were two other car storage services here."

"Built by the will of a great people upon foundations of Michigan's faith in her future."

Gov. G. Mennen Williams was a handsome popular governor at the time of the bridge opening. Here is a commemorative coin of the bridge opening with his picture on one side.

Lester said, "There were 14 gas stations in Mackinaw at that time. We stayed open 24 hours a day. My light bill was $1200 a month. I found out at a Texaco meeting that I sold more gas than anybody north of Bay City. That big double tanker was coming in three times a week (to fill fuel tanks located where Conkling Heritage Park is now). Then the little truck, which carried about 2500 gallons of gas, would come up here in between. They didn't have the interstate completed for the first three years I had the station, so it got to be a regular stop for hundreds of people coming and going. In fact, I saw the same people and watched their kids grow up. As I-75 was completed, there were gas stations put on every exit all the way up. That cut back on my business then and I decided to retire."

The Stokes said they don't remember a lot of noise from the bridge construction. "It was surprisingly quiet for all that riveting and stuff that was done," said Lester.

There is a noise they miss though, Emma said. "Before the bridge was built the fog horn (at the lighthouse) would sing us to sleep, just rattle the building when the horn would go. When the bridge was built, that was the end of the foghorn. They have foghorns out on the bridge now that we don't hear."

Lester reminisced about other things he and Emma miss from times prior to the bridge being part of the landscape. "Before the bridge was built we had a little park down by the fort. There were bear cages, fox, owls, wildcats, and coons," he said. He told about the pavilion, located on Huron Avenue just under the bridge.

"After we were married we went in there for dances," said Emma.

"The hay fever people used that every year," Lester chimed in. "They had dances and card parties. They entertained in there pretty near every night."

There was so much demand for fuel that Marathon had many large tanks of fuel which were filled by freighter. These sat where Conkling Heritage Park is today.

Hay fever people? Lester explained: "They'd come up about Memorial Day. People came all summer long with tents and occasionally a homemade trailer they'd put in the park, down by the lighthouse. They came because of the good air up here. They got relief from their hay fever. They were choking and coughing. One lady from Indiana came up here. Her husband had carried her out of her house, set her in the car, drove up here, and carried her out of the car into one of the cabins that my folks had. She stayed there for hay fever and by the time the season was over her health was back. She came for years after that. She worked for Alice (at Alice's Kandy and Korn) for years."

"Then they finally got enough medicines that really helped the hay fever," said Emma. "The people didn't have to leave home and come up here."

Camping at Old Mackinac Point lighthouse

But that didn't happen before the Stokes family reaped the benefits of the "hay fever people." "That's where my oldest son met his wife," said Lester. "She was a friend of one of the families who came up here for hay fever."

Their son, Keith, has learned to love the Mackinac Bridge like so many others who have Mackinaw City connections. He is a photographer who has taken and sold many pictures of the bridge. Whenever he visits his parents, he finds his way down to the bridge.

"He's walked the bridge several times," Lester said. "He walked it three times on one Labor Day. He likes walking."

Local entrepreneurs weren't the only ones trying to start a business to make money off of the new workers. At the time of this letter the Michigan Central Railroad owned all of the south side of Central Ave. Fourth Street, mentioned in this letter, is now Nicolet St.

Grand Rapids Mich. January 8 1954.

File L-22139-Mackinaw City, Mich.

Mackinaw City, Mich. – Proposed lease to C. Frederick Curtis.

H.H.Vaughn,
Ft. ayne (sic), Ind.

Referring further to our letter December 21st, and your letter of December 15th, relative to request of C.Frederick Curtis, V.P. of the First National Bank of Petoskey, Mich. , to lease parcel of property in Mackinaw City, to create a branch bank.

We have contacted Mr. Curtis relative to the above and find it is their idea to establish this branch bank to provide banking services for contractors and bridge workers if and when the stratis bridge is build.

Also they are required to erect bank in Emmit (sic) County and as Fourth Street in Mackinaw City is the dividing line between Emmit and Cheboygan Counties they would be required to have space west of Fourth Street.

However due to the uncertainty of just where the bridge will enter Mackinaw City Mr. Curtis asks to hold off on their propose (sic) location until more definit (sic) information is developed, at which time he will get in touch with us.

G. B. Peterson.

CC: M. Miller, Bldg.
CC: F. Bd Good, Detroit, Mich.
CC. Abant, Mackinaw City, Mich.
CC: Harry Bill. Cadillac, Mich.

ENTREPRENEUR

Where would hundreds of workers live for the three years it would take to build the Mackinac Bridge? Clem Valot, local businessman, wondered the same thing. "I told my wife that they're going to spend $100 million to build this bridge and Mackinaw City is only a little tiny town. St. Ignace is a little tiny

Shirley and Clem Valot. Her wedding gown was made from the fabric of his WWII parachute.

town. If you were in business at that time, you would certainly have a good opportunity to build a business and succeed at it because you'd have a lot of customers. This is one reason why we left Cheboygan and came to Mackinaw City."

The bridge plans soon became reality and workers entered town to begin their labors. "I had a (Gulf) service station that we ran 24 hours a day," Clem said. "The first ones we had come into the station were Charlie and Margaret Sherwood, a young married couple who lived in Lakeland, Florida. They had this little trailer they drove all the way up here. They got here in the middle of March when the snow banks were about ten to fifteen feet high. They pulled into my gas station and said, 'We came here to build a bridge. Where can we park our trailer?' I said, 'There's no place open. The only thing we've got right now are state parks but you can only stay in there fifteen days then you have to move. We have no private parks.' Charlie said, 'We want to stay here three years or more. What should we do?' This couple had used just about all the money they had to get to Mackinaw City. I suppose the only thing they had left to do was to write back to their mother or dad, or somebody, to try to get enough money to get back to Florida. Neither one of them had ever seen snow, so you can imagine what it was like coming into Mackinaw City under these kinds of conditions. I saw that they were a couple in distress, so I told them, 'You can park right alongside my gas station. I will run an electric line out to you. My bathrooms are on the outside and you can get good drinking water there. The bathrooms are heated and you can use them for your toilets.' So Charlie looked at me—now this is one Rebel looking at a Yankee—and said, 'What's that going to cost me?' I said, 'If you will look me in the eye and promise you will not use my electricity to heat your trailer, I'll charge you a dollar a day.' He said, 'We think we'll take you up on your offer.' Later on in April the smelt started to run and I believe that he and his wife lived on smelt sandwiches for breakfast, dinner, and supper.

"The bridge developed more and more, and more people were coming in with trailers and nobody had a place to go. I got in connection with Jack Kenville who lived next door to me (on Lake Street) and on our three lots of ground we built fourteen trailer spaces and filled them almost instantly. We set up a laundry in Jack's basement for them. We gave them sewer, water, and electricity. We put in a septic tank for each one of them. We charged these people $30 a month. Most of them stayed with us three years or better. Charlie and Margaret Sherwood probably became some of our closest friends. In 1957 they said, 'You've been taking care of us now for the last three years. We want you and your wife to come down to Florida and we're going to show you what Florida is like.' So my wife (Shirley) and I started going to Florida in 1957."

Clem's early experience as a campground operator served him well. He later built two more in the area. The second one was located on South Nicolet Street. "We had public fishing there. You could come in and catch a fish and my wife would cook it. We had paddleboat rides and a restaurant. I could get in about 110 campsites there."

After his campground was purchased by water park developers, Clem went a mile and half farther south of town on Nicolet and built yet another campground, this one smaller. "It has an employment of one, and that's me," Clem said with a laugh. "I mow about ten acres. You can get all of the hookups in there. You have to register yourself and it's $15 a night. You put your money in the can. I have a walking trail where you can enjoy sheep, llama, rabbits, and fishing, and that all goes with the $15.

"I'm eighty years old and I just started a rabbit farm," Clem said. "Since I can remember, coming as a kid off the farm, I started to work and I haven't quit since."

Clem shares that strong work ethic with his fellow Mackinaw City residents, many of whom come from families that have lived here from the time the bridge was built and even before.

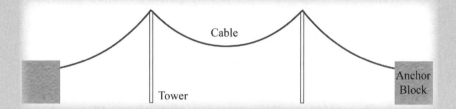

Cable

Tower

Anchor
Block

The bridge consists of two towers which you might think of as two Paul Bunyans standing firmly on bedrock. These 552-foot tall giants hold the cables on their shoulders. The ends of the cables are locked securely in the anchor blocks. From these cables dangle the roadbed.

The cables are 24-1/2 inches in diameter, far too heavy to be floated out to the bridge and installed. So the cables were actually constructed, in place, on the bridge. This process is called spinning. In this photo, taken from the anchor block looking down the length of the bridge, you can see the spinning in process.

Men at the bottom are anchoring the strands of the cable while men along the catwalk are making sure the strands have just the right tension.

Joe Fletcher

"What Precision!"

Mackinaw City resident Ken Teysen knows about the who, where, when, why, and how the Mackinac Bridge was built and can recite facts and figures pertaining to the years before its construction.

"My memory of the first year is that there was a lot of activity, a lot of material brought here, nearly a thousand men at work," Ken recalled. "Not initially, but when things happened above the water for the next three years, there were a thousand men at work. You could look out and not see one, they were so tiny. If there were workmen climbing or spinning the cables you couldn't really see them."

Tourists and locals alike were trying to keep up with the bridge's construction, but the distance from shore was too great to see the workmen. Because of this the Mackinaw City Lions Club saw an opportunity to raise funds. "The Lions Club had some coin operated binoculars," Ken said. "We started by renting four. You put a coin in and it had about a 60-power magnification so then you could see the workers. They were so popular that we ended up buying 12 or 15 of them. We probably took in $7000 or $8000, or more, every summer with no effort on our part except to go get the money. There are still a few of these binoculars around."

Ken Teysen

15

Although Ken did not actually work on the bridge, he explained how precise a project it was: "They had various piers in the water and on the shore. Where (surveying) lines of sight crossed each other, that would be the location of the supporting underwater piers for the two main towers. They were exact to within an eighth of an inch in the construction. The last (supporting) section of the bridge built on shore was put on a barge. It weighed something like 200 tons. It was 60 feet high, very unstable, but they would raise it up here (to meet the existing spans already in place). There were holes on each end for rivets to go in, and the holes fit precisely. That's hard to believe because we're talking about a span 8/10 of a mile. With heat and cold there's contraction and expansion of steel.

The last section of the deck framework was towed to site and then lifted into place.

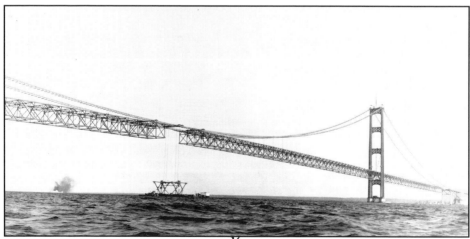

M.J. Duggan, Michigan Dept. of Transportation, Mackinac Bridge Authority

How they could build something on shore and be within an eighth of an inch of where it was supposed to be boggles the mind."

An amateur photographer, Ken took pictures of the bridge as it was being built. He pointed to a framed photo of the bridge on his dining room wall. "The day I took this picture, I was just walking around town taking snapshots," he said. Little did he know that this picture would become well-known in Mackinaw City and all over Michigan. It shows the bridge's towers and cables, but the roadbed is not completed. Ken's photo is a top seller at Teysen's Gallery and was also used on the front of the local Chamber of Commerce brochure.

Eventually the roadbed was finished and when the bridge was being readied to open, Ken was there. "Several people have stated that they were in the first car to drive across the bridge," he said. "I'm not going to dispute that, but the bridge opened November 1, 1957. Two days before that I received a call from downstate saying that NBC News wanted to get a picture of the bridge prior to the opening day. They were sending a reporter and a photographer up and would I take care of them? I said, 'Sure!' so I contacted the Bridge Authority and they were all for it. I had a station wagon at the time. I put the photographer on the tailgate of the wagon. He had his TV camera, tripod, and so forth. I thought I might lose him on the way over so I drove very slowly. The reporter rode up front with me. We crossed the bridge on October 31, which makes me think I was the first one across. Well, things like that don't impress me very much, so whether I was or not doesn't matter. What does matter is that that night, that picture was on NBC News. So it gave the idea of the opening day a boost and encouraged people to come up the next day and be there."

Ken's aptitude for driving across the bridge came in handy again during the first few Labor Day Bridge Walks. Before busses were used to take people to the starting point, Ken and other townspeople offered rides back and forth. "It wasn't organized," he said. "There weren't that many people walking initially, probably a thousand people would have been a lot. I think the Bridge Authority arranged to take people back and forth on one or two busses. After the first few years, somebody had the inspiration and got the legislation passed enabling us to recruit every school bus from Traverse City and Alpena north to take people across, so now we get over a hundred busses to chauffeur people."

Ken recalled some changes the Bridge Walk has seen since its inception. "One year you'd walk from the north side (of the bridge) to the south side, and then the next year from the south side to the north side, for about a 5 or 6 year period. Then somebody came up with a thought that when you walked from north to south, you end up in a town. When you walk from south to north, you're a mile away from town. So the first thing anybody wants after they walk the bridge is something cool to drink. Second thing they want is a place to recycle it. Well, if you're a mile from town, can you wait that long? So they decided that it was just better if the Bridge Walk always goes from north to south."

As interested as Ken has always been in the bridge and everything connected to it, he has never walked across it on Labor Day. "I've walked ON the bridge. I've been out there many times, but I always was too busy passing out ice water. And, of course, Labor Day weekend for our restaurant was the busiest day of our year. We were crazy. I really had to stay fairly close to that. It was exciting. A 900-person village with 50,000 people coming to say 'hello'; it was a challenge. Parking cars was a challenge, finding restrooms and getting porta-potties was a challenge, but it was exciting and still is. So, therefore, I have never walked the bridge. I've probably walked out and back many times longer than the five mile stretch, but I've never officially walked the bridge."

Ken and his wife Betty keep track of the comings and goings on the bridge from windows in their home just blocks from the bridge's approach. "Every year there's been a truckers' convention of sorts up here where they cross the bridge and have exotic lights all over their rigs," Ken said. "If you go down to the end of our block, it's a ringside seat for that."

Like many people who live in Mackinaw City, Ken has a deep respect for the Mackinac Bridge and all it has brought to his village. "If you go up by the park any day in the summer time you'll see several dozen people sitting on benches just looking at the bridge," he said. "It's a very graceful bridge."

Inside the anchor block the strands of the cable are put on "strand shoes" before the wheel is sent back to lay down the next strand.

"THE BRIDGE TOOK OUR HOUSE."

Ron Gwilt was only eight years old when construction started on the bridge, but he has vivid memories of the months before when his childhood home was moved to make way for the approach to the bridge. "Our house used to be on Jamet Street," he recalled. "It actually used to sit underneath the Jamet exit as you're coming south." Ron's family had their home site taken by eminent domain, the right of government to seize private property for public use. The Gwilts were one of 16 families that were in that situation. Ron's parents bought a piece of property on Central Avenue and made arrangements to have their house moved.

"They put the big old I-beams underneath the house," Ron said, "and as it was going down the road, the I-beams broke right in half. They went down and dug into the asphalt. I remember for years I'd go down Central Avenue and those scrape marks would still be in the road. It messed the house up a little bit, made it a little bit crooked. My friends and I were all sitting there watching when it happened. Whoops!" The house eventually was repaired and the Gwilts raised their family in it. Ron's father Mearl and sister Gracy still live there on the corner of Central and Hiawatha west of town.

Mearl worked as a carpenter's helper on the bridge. "I remember taking my dad to work with my mother," Ron said. "She'd pile all four kids into the Studebaker, then head for the worksite. We'd drive up on the ramp built out of plywood and two-by-fours out to where they were working, drop Dad off, then we'd go back and get him at night. He used to walk those eight-inch beams out there and carry two-by-fours and other stuff. He'd talk about that, how he didn't really want to do it, but it was extra pay (for hazardous duty). One guy talked him into doing it, so he tried it and got used to it."

While constructing the roadbed the crew walked the beams.

M.J. Duggan, Michigan Dept. of Transportation, Mackinac Bridge Authority

19

Even though Ron said workers didn't wear safety harnesses back then, his dad never got hurt. "He talked about one guy who fell through and the guy got up and came to work the next day," Ron said. "He just got bruised a little bit.

"At the end of the day if there was something that they didn't want to bring back with them, whoosh! It would just go over the side. Back in the seventies I used to scuba dive and find all kinds of stuff." Things were accidentally dropped into the water, too. Wrenches and pieces of flexible cable with hooks are among the items Ron and his friends found while diving around the piers.

Like most boys in Mackinaw City at the time, Ron enjoyed watching the construction; however, he just looked at it as a run-of-the-mill bridge and didn't realize the significance of the structure. "I wasn't old enough to be impressed," he said. "It's a whole lot bigger deal for me now than it was then. We have a view of it from our house. We can sit in our living room and see it, and we can look at it from our bedroom at night."

Lucky visitors to Ron and wife Linda's home might even be offered a ride in their 20-foot boat to view the bridge close up. "I'll go for a boat ride and just go underneath the bridge. I've done it almost daily for years. But when I take somebody new out there, then I have the same feeling that they have. I'm excited because they haven't been there before. I always take them out so that they can look up and see the structure right smack in the middle. Then I show them the depth of the water underneath. That's a really big thrill for me."

Looking straight up from the water to the bridge. The center lanes are open mesh to reduce wind loads and to allow snow to drop through. Notice the car passing over.

THE BRIDGE QUEEN

Diane Krueger Harvey's sash has faded, but not her memories of being chosen Miss Mackinaw City for the Mackinac Bridge's opening festivities. "I decided at the last minute to try out for Queen of Mackinaw City," Diane said. "I thought, 'I'll just do it.' So I grabbed my yellow chiffon gown, I had some high heels around there someplace, and I went to the school. I was the thirteenth participant. Thirteen has always been lucky for me. I stuck a rabbit's foot down inside my bra, and I ended up being chosen. It was such a kick! This wasn't so much a beauty pageant as it was picking a representative of girls who lived in Mackinaw City at the time."

Diane's mother, Mary Krueger LaCombe, remembers this impulsiveness as being typical of Diane and other young people. "They have to try things," said Mary. "She was always willing to try something new."

Soon Diane was caught up in the excitement that followed: a flurry of activities which included shopping for a dress, a photo session, and hair styling. Because

Diane Krueger Harvey and her mom, Mary Krueger LaCombe

she was only seventeen years old, Diane had to have her chaperone, Peg Darrow, accompany her for all these activities.

"Then we got information that told us 'This is what's going to happen, this is what we'll expect of you," Diane said. She was escorted by an MP from the Army National Guard to each of the activities on her full schedule during the four-day bridge dedication festivities. "Every day for three or four days he'd come and pick me up when I had to go do things—a banquet and several parades. He was really respectful and nice."

"A uniform makes the man," said Mary with a smile. "And he was so kind and patient with us, because lots of times we didn't know where we were going or what time we were supposed to be there and he'd try to help us a lot. We had that Oldsmobile convertible at our disposal."

Their official car was just one of about 90 white Oldsmobile convertibles brought up to the area as transportation for dignitaries and each of the 83 county queens who would attend the ceremonies. "All those white Oldsmobiles," Mary said. "That was beautiful."

Diane waves from her seat on the white Oldsmobile.

Diane remembers the special dress she wore. "I was wearing my white dress, an organza, really pretty, a lot of underskirts, and little blue flowers were scattered throughout the dress with little green leaves on it. I think I wore that dress for everything I did. The parade I remember most is the one here in Mackinaw City. The city doesn't look anything like it did then. It was really a small town, but it was a big deal. Going across the bridge was wonderful. What a thrill in that convertible!"

"We had to go across the bridge four times in one day so they could take pictures," Mary recalled. "They had some music down at the pavilion and I remember Governor Williams taking two or three steps with the women (including Diane) so they could say they danced with the governor."

"A lot of things I've just forgotten about," said Diane, "but the biggest thing I remember is riding in that convertible and how my face got tired from smiling so much."

The dignitaries at the opening of the Mackinac Bridge. G. Mennen Williams is the tall man in the dark overcoat. To his right is Dr. David Steinman, engineer of the Bridge.

23

Mary recalls the goodwill created by all the bridge festivities. "Everybody was friendly with each other," she said. "The businessmen all went out of their way to make their businesses look nice. It seemed like everybody was so happy that the bridge was being finished. It was just a good time."

Diane is now retired from nursing and lives in Rockford, Michigan. She gets back up to Mackinaw City about six times a year and always makes a stop at the bridge. "No matter which way I come into town," she said, "it's always good to see the bridge. I love to see it when it's lit up at night. There's just something about seeing that bridge that feels special because it was a special time in my life. It brings a little tingle. I was part of that once, a long, long time ago."

This was the Oldsmobile advertisement used in the Bridge celebration.

"I KNEW IF I WAS GOING TO HAVE ANYTHING I'D HAVE TO WORK FOR IT."

Dick and Nancy (Dagwell) Campbell both have lifelong ties to Mackinaw City. Their home on Huron Avenue is on the same site as the house in which Nancy grew up. Her family ran the Marine Reporting Station there from 1900 to 1970. Dick came to Mackinaw City in 1940 when his father was stationed at Old Mackinac Point Lighthouse just down the road. Although they left Mackinaw City for a while to go to college and the military, they found their way back when Dick got a job working on the car ferries that carried automobiles back and forth between the upper and lower peninsulas. "It was a good job, working on the boats," Dick said.

"I loved the ferries," said Nancy. "I used to ride them a lot because I took piano lessons over in St. Ignace. So every week, year round, I would be riding the ferry over to St. Ignace."

Speaking of the *Chief Wawatam* and the *Ste. Marie*, two of the larger ferries, Dick said, "When they left the dock, they left a cloud of smoke. You couldn't see the street out there through the smoke. In the summer time, everybody's washing (hung on clotheslines) was always covered with black soot from the smoke. It was just unbelievable, the black smoke that would be belching out of those boats, going right up the main street (Central Avenue)."

Eventually construction was begun on the Mackinac Bridge and things changed for the Campbell family. Their son loved watching the earthmoving vehicles as they built the approach to the bridge. "Kids used to sit by the hour up there under that tree watching the equipment," said Dick.

"That would be where Indian Pathways Park is today," said Nancy. "They moved all those homes out and built the approach."

Nancy taught school during this time and Dick took a second job as bridge construction was stepped up. "I always worked two jobs," he said. "You'd get a good 16 hours every day, working on your regular job and working elsewhere. I'm a product of the Depression so I knew if I was going to have anything, I'd have to work for it. I wanted to live here and my wife's from here. That's what we wanted, so we had to do it."

Dick's second job was "loading, unloading and transporting for the general contractor for the underwater bridge piers up until they got to the steel," he said. "All of the concrete and a lot of other materials came in by train and truck here and were loaded off the dock where Shepler's is now onto barges and taken out to be used on the bridge. At times you'd see half a dozen barges or tugs down here underneath the dock. They worked 24 hours a day, weather permitting. It was a big operation going on here for quite some time. It was a big boost to the economy because they paid well compared to other places. There were hoards of workers. They would come and go. Some of those people thought they were going to make their stake working here building the bridge, like during the Gold Rush. They weren't experienced, so they came, then they'd leave, and next week there would be more show up. There was a big turnover of people. There were an awful lot of ironworkers. They started the steel work after the underwater job was done. That was a really big job."

Dick and Nancy Campbell with some of Dick's maritime treasures

26

The Vacationland was the last automobile ferry to serve the Straits

Nancy recalled, "The day the bridge opened was also the day that was the last run of the ferries. We were standing down there watching the last boat move out. I cried. A lot of people worked on the boats. It took a lot of people out of town." When the car ferries stopped running, many people left town for jobs elsewhere.

Dick said, "With the ferry system alone, there were about 450 employees. But most of the people were absorbed into other state jobs if they wanted to go. The day the bridge opened was my first day of work up there (working for the Bridge Authority), and that was my last day of work on the ferries. I went from one job to the other just like that."

From changing light bulbs at the top of the towers to diving underneath the water—all these tasks were performed by Dick. "I worked in the maintenance department," he explained. "I was a diver, a steeplejack, and under those classifications you get just about everything. We plowed snow in the winter and did painting in the summer. I've covered every inch (of the bridge) one way or another, either on a scaffold, or climbing, or whatever. Each year we made the annual inspection of the underwater piers. Every one of the piers was inspected from the water all the way down to the bottom of the pier for any damage and changes there might be. The deepest water was 120 feet. We used all different kinds of diving equipment. We used the old hard helmets and we used the scuba. I got my training there and I did commercial diving on my own after I retired."

This work came naturally to Dick, but he knew it was risky. "I grew up in a lighthouse with my father," he said. "I lived on the water all my life. Any time you go in that water, it's a risk. The old saying is, 'The water is always out to get you,' so you've got to be on guard constantly. One slip and that's it. I was in commercial fishing for quite a few years, so between lighthouses, bridges, commercial fishing and diving, the water has been my whole life."

At the same time he was working for the Bridge Authority, Dick went together with a group of people and purchased one of the old car ferries, the one they use for the vesper cruises today. "We formed what was called Straits Transit Company. We purchased the dock down where Arnold Transit runs out of now. We were in business quite a few years, running to Mackinac Island. Eventually we sold out to Arnold Transit. That was a very good move on our part. Most of them (his partners) were much older than I was and it made a very nice retirement for them. My plan was someday, when I retired (from the Bridge Authority), I would work on our ferries. But the sale came along and that's the way it went."

Although Dick and Nancy have spent much of their lives within a stone's throw of the Mackinac Bridge, one thing they've never participated in is the Labor Day Bridge Walk. Nancy said, "I always had to go to school the next day, so I didn't feel like it."

Dick said he'd walked the bridge enough in his work. "I walked it up and down and crossways," he said with a smile. Preparing for the Bridge Walk was also part of his job. "We would start two or three weeks in advance making signs, setting up barricades, getting publications, and after it was over we'd take

The Bridge authority crew sets up all of the equipment
that makes the Bridge Walk run smoothly

another two weeks to pick up all the junk and store it for the next year. We'd get up at three o'clock in the morning to go to work all day. So, to this day, I just stay right away from it."

From the expansive picture windows in their living room, the Campbells have a wonderful view of the bridge. "It's really great," said Dick, who echoes the sentiments of many Mackinaw City residents, "to think that I'm lucky enough to be here to enjoy it all these years. I have people come here and look out that window and say, 'If I lived here, I'd never leave.'"

Spinning the cable along side of the bridge. You are looking down into the anchor block.

"I WAS ALWAYS TOO BUSY TO WALK THE BRIDGE."

As a seventeen-year-old, Dorothy Phillips Krueger spent the summer of 1957 working at her aunt's restaurant. "It was a small place called Jane's that had about five tables, all (rustic looking) Rittenhouse," Dorothy recalled. Jane's, one of many small restaurants in town, was located on the bustling south end of Mackinaw City near the state car ferry dock.

"At the restaurant we served chili, homemade soup, burgers, malts, fries, BLTs and other sandwiches like tuna and egg salad, and the daily specials just for the workers," she said. "The pork chop special was really great. Aunt Jane was a smoker and had a habit of smoking the cigarette right down to the filter without taking it out of her mouth and breaking off the ash. There used to be bets as to whether she would lose the ash as she was flipping hamburgers, but she never did. There was a jukebox and a shuffleboard table and a photo wall. The regulars would give her a picture of themselves and she would put it on the wall."

Dorothy remembers the bridge workers who came into the restaurant as polite and friendly. "They were great guys, never a problem," she said. "I had a couple of dates with a guy named John. We went to the movies in Cheboygan and to the drive-in for a snack. I also went to the fair with him. He was a great guy, very polite, but there was no spark. I met my future husband (Ken) about that time and I was more interested in him."

Future jobs for Dorothy prevented her from ever being part of the Bridge Walk festivities. "Labor Day is an extra-hours work day and I never had it off in over 35 years," she said. "No one living in town above the age of 14 and under the age of 80 ever has Labor Day off. We have to make hay while the sun shines— it's a long winter!"

View of towers and roadbed from the water.

"THE BRIDGE IS ESPECIALLY BEAUTIFUL AT NIGHT."

In 1941 Jane McLott stepped off the train, three young children in tow, intending to make Mackinaw City her home. Jane remembers, "I lived in Royal Oak then. My neighbor used to come up here and tell me how beautiful it was and about the water, how you could see so far, and how the snow was so white. I decided that's where I wanted to live." After checking out the area while on vacation, Jane made up her mind to do just that. In the years to come she opened a beauty shop and became a church organist.

Jane saw many changes during the time of the Mackinac Bridge's construction. "The town was really busy for three years, day and night, cars coming and going all the time," she said. "I did the hair of a secretary who worked in the office at the center of the bridge and she introduced me to an engineer." Jane was single at the time and dated this engineer, one of several who worked on the bridge. "He was nice to go out to dinner with," she said. "He invited me to cross the bridge even though it was before it was (officially) opened. He took me over in a worker's truck, we got off on the other side, then we came back. He asked me, 'Do you know what you just did? You're the first one to cross the bridge, get off on the other side, and come right back, but let's not put it in the paper.'" (He was referring to newspaper accounts of the previous crossing of Millie Cole, a celebrated local citizen who was known as the first to cross the bridge.) Jane

Mary Lou Peters

Jane McLott

said, "Millie crossed it first, but she didn't come right back. They left her over there till midnight until somebody could bring her back."

After Jane's chauffeur/engineer was done with his job here he moved on to another work assignment. "When he left here he went to Phnom Penh (Cambodia). We corresponded for quite a long time after he went to build another bridge there."

Jane enjoys the panoramic view of the Mackinac Bridge from her home on Huron Avenue. Next to Jane's house is a small city park, one of several in Mackinaw City, where visitors may take advantage of the scenery. She described the development of the park: "Originally that was the end of a city street. The cars used to come down here and park. They were always waking us up in the middle of the night because they got stuck in the sand. So the city turned it into a park. There are a lot of people who come down to the park, even in the winter. They're very interesting to watch. They have reunions down there with the old folks and the young folks. They play games and have a good time. They're not destructive; they're just usually enjoying the view. Everybody appreciates it."

Jane's expansive view includes Mackinac Island, St. Ignace, and all the freighters and other water traffic on the Straits. "All of Shepler's ferries come right here and turn in front of our house," she said. "It's fun to watch."

The bridge holds special memories for Jane, not only of her first crossing, but of good times with friends and family who also appreciate the beauty of the bridge. "When my children come to visit, they have a bonfire that usually lasts till dawn," she said. "The bridge is such a beautiful thing, especially at night. Sometimes the lights are reflected right to the shore, a duplicate of the bridge. So beautiful."

Sandy Planisek

32

Proud Ironworker

J.C. Stilwell, or "Jaybird" as he was called by his fellow ironworkers, is well-known in Mackinaw City as a builder of the Mackinac Bridge. "I started out as apprentice, went in the bolt-up gang—that's putting the bolts in the bridge—then I went on setting iron and spinning the cable and doing all kinds of work. Anything there was to do, we did it. We were making about $300 a week take home pay. We were only making $3.50 an hour, but overtime was double time, that's $7.00 an hour. That was unheard of downtown in Mackinaw where they were making about $1.50 an hour. We didn't have much time off, except when the weather was bad. It was usually so cold I wore long underwear, even in the summer."

J. C. Stilwell under a photo of himself in front of the bridge

J.C. looks back on his years of bridge work as some of his best. "I am proud to be an ironworker, proud to be on the Mackinac Bridge. I met the nicest men in the world. They're good men, hard men. They fight hard and they work hard. They get mad at each other, but the higher they go in the air, the softer they get. I'd give my eyeteeth to go back to work on that bridge right now."

There were some difficult times though, such as the day a catwalk collapsed and two men died. J.C. related his eyewitness account: "It looked like slow motion. The guys were falling in air. I can close my eyes and still see them." A friend of J.C.'s was in the St. Ignace trailer park where one of the accident victims was staying and relayed a story to J.C.: "The night of the accident you could hear his wife crying and wailing all night in the trailer park for her husband. They tell me they can still hear her."

J. C.'s hard hat used to hang in the Bridge museum

He remembers the circumstances surrounding the deaths of all five of the men who died during the construction of the bridge. But one story of a worker being buried in the bridge's concrete is simply not true, according to J.C. "It's a story that started and it just kind of mushroomed," he said. "I don't know where it came from. We had a guy who dropped his foot in the concrete and we pulled him out, but there's nobody buried in that concrete. In fact, when we poured concrete, the concrete was poured in a different way. There wasn't a lot of loose concrete.

"But it was dangerous work," he continued. "The first week on the job there were so many accidents. I asked myself, 'What did I get into?' It looked like a meat wagon! Before I left for work, I'd kiss my kids because I thought I might never see them again."

Perhaps the dangerous nature of working high up in the air on a structure of steel builds the camaraderie that inspired J.C. to organize the first Ironworkers Festival in Mackinaw City—an event that is well-attended by ironworkers and their families each summer. Some of J.C.'s co-workers from 50 years ago are among them. The weekend's fun contests are the same as the tasks J.C.

and his buddies used to perform on the bridge. Now they're done by younger men. "They climb up poles, throw rivets, tie knots, tie rods, and climb columns," he said. "It's awesome. They're about the same way as we used to be. They're proud to be ironworkers. Usually they're sons of ironworkers, so it's bred right into them."

J.C.'s Mackinac Bridge Museum above Mama Mia's restaurant in

Mackinaw City, filled with artifacts from the bridge construction era, was a favorite place for tourists, local residents, and ironworkers' families to learn about the bridge, but a fire in 2005 ended that opportunity. "Everything burned," said J.C. "Everything." The long room was filled with hard hats, tools, pictures, and memories. "It's hard for me," he said sadly. "I can't talk about it. I spent 30 years putting that together. I

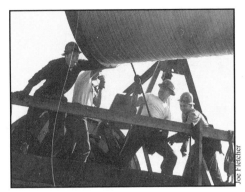

Men at work on the Bridge

started the museum in 1980. I didn't have anything to start with, just a book. As the years went by, I put it together and ironworkers from all over the country brought me stuff. I had all kinds of things in there and they all had stories connected with them."

Fortunately, J.C. had stored some of the things that were dearest to him at home: a program from the bridge dedication, a wrench, and many framed photos. Some of these will be used as part of his personal museum, the Mackinac Bridge Men Museum, dedicated to the hardworking guys who were his friends and co-workers. "These ironworkers were the finest men in the country," he boasted. "They're what they call bridge men. When you say, 'There's a bridge man,' that's the top of the line." The new museum will be housed on his property south of town and he hopes to have it open soon.

J.C. often goes to the foot of the bridge just to gaze at the bridge and remember his special time as part of the crew that built the magnificent structure. "If I had it to do all over again, I'd go right back there and do the same thing," he said. "You can't imagine how many souls and how many men touched each other going through. When you're up on the tower it's a beautiful view. You can stand up there and look and it's just gorgeous, gorgeous, gorgeous. And every time I go over this bridge it gives me a chill."

A bridge worker

9/29/56

The Bridge tower stands 552 feet above water level. You can really appreciate that height from this photo taken before the roadbed was installed.

"*Of course, we named her Bridget.*"

What would you name a baby girl who was born on the same day as the groundbreaking ceremony for the Mackinac Bridge? Bridget, of course! "She was born on May 7, 1954," said her mother, Jean Paquet. "We were wondering what to name her. She was the fifth one (in a family of fourteen children). We were running out of names. We talked to different people and they thought we should name her Bridget, so that's how she got her name."

At age three, Bridget rode in the dedication day parade in a convertible driven by her father, the late Bill Paquet. Jean recalled, "Her dress was white with a green sash. She still has the dress. It was special to her." A couple of months later Bridget appeared in a newspaper photo as they celebrated the one millionth car to cross the Mackinac Bridge.

The bridge still holds a special place in Bridget's heart. She travels to Mackinaw City from her home in Kalamazoo often and when she does, she

Jean Paquet holding a photo of herself with her husband Bill and daughter Bridget

always finds time to take a walk down by the bridge. Jean said that Bridget has missed the Labor Day Bridge Walk only once since she walked it for the first time at age eight. Bridget has plans to attend the bridge's 50th Bridge Walk, this time with many of her brothers, sisters, nieces, and nephews. "We usually have a big gang here for Labor Day weekend," said Jean. "Most of our kids want to come to walk the bridge so it's going to be quite a day."

The Paquet family was raised in a house on Etherington Street just a block from the bridge approach. For years Jean's children had a tradition of setting up a lemonade stand to sell drinks to thirsty walkers. Now that tradition has been passed on to the next two generations. "My kids used to do anything to earn a dollar, which helped our big family," Jean said with a smile. "The kids sold lemonade and last year they (the grandkids) also put up a special sign. They were raising money for the soldiers over in Iraq. They took in $80 to send some packages over to them. My son, Barry, is in Iraq."

Jean said that she and her family also take part in the Fort Michilimackinac Pageant on Memorial Day, making it a four-generation affair. "Bridget always takes part in the pageant. She's a French Colonial lady. Her children usually take part, and her grandchildren, too. A lot of my grandkids like to come up and be in the pageant."

Strong family ties for the Paquet family go way back. Jean remembers no jealousy from brothers and sisters as Bridget got lots of attention for her Mackinac Bridge connection through the years. "I think they were excited because of it," said Jean. "You could go any place and people would say, 'Oh, you're the one who had the little girl named Bridget!'"

Georgianna Ranville Clark, Diane Krueger, and Bridget Paquet

FROM HOT DOGS TO LIFE-SIZE CARVINGS

 Before the Mackinac Bridge was constructed, car ferries carried traffic back and forth across the Straits of Mackinac. Jerry Prior's grandparents owned a small restaurant (the Jerry Lee, named for their grandson) near the ferry dock. "They sold hot dogs, sandwiches, and hamburgers," Jerry remembered. "I started selling hot dogs out the back end. I was able to get hot dogs fifteen to the pound. I sold them on the dock for twenty cents a pound. I think I sold half a ton one summer." Jerry was still in high school and considered his job a steppingstone to his life's career as a restaurant owner. "My friends were working down at the gas station for $30 or $35 a week. That would be my worst income day on the dock. I'd make over a hundred dollars a day on the weekend. I made a lot of money on the docks."

Jerry Prior in front of his collection of ferry boat pictures

Later Jerry became somewhat of an entrepreneur when he bought a little trailer for $1000 and set it up at the end of the dock. "I sold hot dogs and caramel corn out on the docks," he said. "I made my own caramel corn, the first caramel corn in town." He could see his future in the restaurant business and had an idea that he might eventually take over his grandparents' restaurant. "But my granddad got so sick of it that he sold it. That kind of pulled the rug out from underneath me."

So Jerry went to work for the state ferry system as a deckhand on the big boats that carried people and their cars between the upper and lower peninsulas. "I could have made it

Jerry at the hot dog stand

a lifetime career being on the boats," Jerry said. "You wouldn't get rich or anything, but you'd make a good living." His new career came to a halt with the completion of the Mackinac Bridge. Ferries would no longer be needed to handle the traffic between Mackinaw City and St. Ignace. Like many people in the small communities around the Straits area, Jerry's life changed dramatically. He and other displaced workers were offered new jobs by the State of Michigan.

"The state would replace everyone," he remembered. "They'd put some on the bridge—toll takers and maintenance. Some went into gravel inspecting. I went down to Lansing, to the design department because I had experience there. I designed roads—intersections, sewers, and setting the grades for the curb and gutters."

Jerry was able to use his art and drafting background in his new work that took him on the road frequently. His lifelong woodcarving hobby was born during one such trip. Jerry recalled, "I'd get into camp in the afternoon, get all set up, and I didn't have anything to do for the evening. We happened to be at Gatlinburg and they had a woodcarving show. I found a subject there I wanted to do, so that's what started me. Little things. Then gradually I got into doing bigger sculptures up here." Those "bigger sculptures" are the ones that can be seen all around Mackinaw City: lifesize wooden images of people important to the village's history. "I did six for the city," Jerry said, "Chief Wawatam,

Alexander Henry, Major DePeyster, Edgar Conkling, Perry Darrow, and I just did Hattie Stimpson. She isn't completed yet, but hopefully she'll be done this summer."

Like many area citizens, Jerry is actively involved in the community. He speaks highly of local leadership in the time of personal and commercial upheaval with the bridge's construction. "I think most people thought when the bridge was finished, everyone would be going right on by," he said. "Mackinaw would become a ghost town. Instead, it just prospered. I think it was the (city) fathers: the (Village) Council and just enough old-fashioned, genuine wanting to get ahead. The Council worked with the business people and they had great ideas. It's more prosperous now than when the (ferry) boats were here."

These days Jerry lives with his wife, Sandy, just blocks from the Mackinac Bridge, which he considers a great feat of engineering. "I've said many times as I've gone across, it's one of the most beautiful, scenic places in the state. Once you get on top you can see all over. It's a great, great thing," he declared.

Jerry carving Mackinaw City's founder Edgar Conkling

Coming Full Circle

In the fall of 1956, Tom Peters was part of a crew that came to St. Ignace to construct a set of jet fuel storage tanks for Kinross Air Force Base. This was tough work for a seventeen-year-old, but typical for laborers back then. "We usually worked from daylight till dark, 16 to 18 hours a day," Tom recalled. "We stayed at a little motel up on the hill in St. Ignace that overlooked the bridge. Every day we'd look to see what had changed on its construction from the day before."

As his job neared completion, Tom and his buddies had a surprise, courtesy of another construction crew. Tom remembers, "One day some ironworkers let us walk a little way out onto the bridge so we could look at it close up. What a thrill! Such a beautiful thing!"

Tom's job ended the day of the opening ceremonies of the bridge dedication. "They told us we had to be out of our motel rooms the day before the grand opening," he said. "Our rooms were already rented for the opening. They had been rented out a year in advance. So we loaded our stuff up and we took the last car ferry boat across as the opening ceremonies for the bridge started."

With the new bridge open for traffic, why didn't his construction crew drive across? "I don't imagine they'd have wanted us to go across the bridge," Tom laughed. "We threw everything we owned on the trucks and looked like a caravan of gypsies. That wouldn't have looked too good coming across the bridge."

Never did he think that fifty years in the future he'd be living near Mackinaw City, be able to see the bridge every day, and cross it whenever he wanted to. "I think it's one of the most magnificent feats of engineering man has ever completed," he said.

Tom now enjoys spending his free time being a sidewalk superintendent to construction projects around Mackinaw City. But when he crosses the bridge with his grandchildren, he proudly shows them the storage tanks that still stand in the St. Ignace harbor.

"THERE'S OUR CAR!"

A long-time supporter of the Mackinaw Area Historical Society, Mary Margaret Cosens was sitting in the audience at a monthly meeting listening to Ken Teysen's program. She remembers, "Ken had a picture of the Mackinac Bridge sitting on an easel and I looked at that and I said, 'Oh, my goodness! There's our car! And there's my husband!'"

The photograph that Mary Margaret referred to was taken by Ken Teysen, a local amateur photographer (see his story in this book.) Mary Margaret and her first husband, Lloyd Thiel, had gone down to the park (now called Alexander Henry Park) to check on the progress of the bridge construction. She remained inside the car, never imagining that 50 years later she would see that day captured in a photo that is now well-known throughout the state of Michigan.

"Every Sunday when we came to church (from their home in Carp Lake, six miles south of Mackinaw City), we would come early so we could look out at

Mary Maragaret (Seelinger Thiel) Cosens

43

the bridge to see what they'd done from one week to the next, see if we could tell the difference," she said. "Everybody would just look and talk about it. It was something a lot of local people did. It was interesting and fun watching that being built."

Mary Margaret remembers a special opportunity offered by the Bridge Authority in the week following the dedication ceremony. "They said that anybody who wanted to go across the bridge for the first time could go free if they had kids in the car. We didn't have any kids, but there was a boy standing along the side of the road. We didn't know him and he didn't know us. We said, 'Come on, do you want to go across the bridge?' So he got in the car with us. Away we went across the bridge and back again. And, we got to go across the bridge free."

Mary Margaret's second husband, Archie Cosens (now deceased), worked on the car ferries that went back and forth between Mackinaw City and St. Ignace. "He worked himself up to being third mate," she said. "He enjoyed that. It was his life, right there, up on the boats." When the bridge was built there was no longer a need for this slower mode of transportation, so the boats were discontinued and Archie was displaced. Mary Margaret remembers: "After the last trip over, he got right off the boat and got right up to taking money for the bridge. He didn't like it though. He said it was amazing how rude some people were. It was expensive when they first started. The fare was high ($3.25 for a car) and people would swear at him, even though it wasn't his fault. So he went to the post office to work."

Labor Day weekends have been exciting for Mary Margaret, even though she has never done the Bridge Walk. She and Archie were volunteer ticket sellers for the bus ride for a few years. "Then we handed out certificates at the end of the Bridge Walk," she said. "I enjoyed that. We got to meet all those people who were excited to be on the bridge and they were real tickled to get those certificates."

For Mary Margaret there's no more standing for hours on the bridge. Now on Labor Day weekends she rolls silverware at the Pancake Chef, a restaurant on Central Avenue where she used to be a waitress. She lives right down the street from the park where her first husband and car were immortalized in that famous photo taken on a Sunday morning so long ago.

Every time she walks out of her house she sees the bridge. "It's just part of the scenery," she laughed. "It's magnificent when you get up there and look around."

"*Dad Crossed the Bridge on His Hands and Knees.*"

Before the Mackinac Bridge was built, Melva Thompson Fosmore was among the Mackinaw City youngsters who sold candy bars, popcorn, coffee, and postcards to passengers in the long lines of cars waiting for ferries to take them across the Straits during deer season. She recalled how cars would be backed up for miles down US23, some of them having waited in line all night long. As the drivers approached town, she would be waiting with her offerings from the snack bar that her folks ran near the State Dock.

"You couldn't haul food down there fast enough," she said. "Some of us didn't go home for two or three days during deer season. We'd even wash their car windows for tips."

When the bridge construction was announced, her husband Cliff (now deceased) was hired as a laborer, one of a crew that did many kinds of work. "Everybody who could work worked on the bridge because the money was so good," Melva said. "Cliff cut trees down for the approach. He had a tree fall on him but, because the ground was swampy, he just sunk down and didn't get hurt. Once a big pipe fell on him and tore the toe right off the rubber boot he was wearing." Once again, no injury.

"They were a good bunch of guys," she said of Cliff's fellow workers. "They all got along."

Cars lined up to get on the dock to board car ferry to cross the Straits before the opening of the bridge.

45

Working on the roadbed of the bridge

Melva's father, Glenn Thompson (now deceased), also had a hand in building the bridge. He was part of the crew that laid the plywood base of the highway before the concrete was poured. "He always said he went across the bridge on his hands and knees," she laughed.

Melva still misses the car ferries and her frequent trips across the Straits. She often went for a ferry ride just for the fun of it, either to St. Ignace or to Mackinac Island. "I love the water," she said. "I'd wait for the waves to get high and run down and hop on the boat. The small boats were best because it seemed like you were right inside the waves." Melva laughed when remembering that she and other local kids thought they were sneaking onto the boats, but found out later the ferry operators knew all along what was going on. "They knew we just wanted to have a good time," she said.

Later in her life Melva made weekly business trips across the bridge to the Upper Peninsula. "I like the bridge," she said. "It's a nice ride across and back. I think about how much the town has changed since the bridge went in."

The line of cars actually on the dock waiting for the auto ferry

"THE BRIDGE IS MY FRIEND."

In the early 1950s Peg Smith and her partner in a large Detroit public relations firm were faced with the governor's challenge of coming up with a plan for a dramatic opening for the Mackinac Bridge.

"We had been trying to figure out what Soapy (the nickname of Governor G. Mennen Williams) could do," Peg said. He'd wanted something unique and the PR firm was having a difficult time finding just the right angle. Ribbon cutting alone just wouldn't do.

A serendipitous phone call to their office proved to be just what they'd been looking for. The International Walkers Association in Chicago proposed that they lead off a walking event to coincide with the bridge opening. When her partner told her of his rejection of "those people from Chicago," Peg told him, "Jim, that's it!"

A mass of humanity is walking south on the right lane of the bridge.

Mackinac Bridge Authority

"So it was really the International Walkers who had the idea of walking the bridge to open it," Peg said.

That first Bridge Walk involved about 60 walkers, many from the International Walkers Association. Some continued to take part for many years. Since 1958 there have been up to 70,000 people of all ages, and from many places in the world, who make the trek over the five-mile span each year on Labor Day.

"The International Walkers sold embroidered patches for walkers to commemorate their achievement," Peg recalled, "and many of the retailers in Mackinaw City created their own patch designs. But I didn't do a patch for my shop, Sign of the Copper Lantern. The International Walkers and I knew each other so they brought me theirs to sell.

"It was always a very busy time and for a number of years I hired extra help on Labor Day weekend," Peg continued. "One year the former owner, Bill Morway, was talked into helping at the store so I could escort his wife Sylvia, who was not well, so she could fulfill her wish to walk across the bridge. She died shortly after."

Another year Peg had a miniature poodle as a companion on the Bridge Walk. She demonstrated how she carried the dog: "I didn't want her to break her foot in the mesh on the walkway, so I just tucked her under one arm and nobody said anything." On today's Bridge Walks pets are not allowed to accompany walkers.

Peg lives in a house overlooking the Straits of Mackinac where she has a view of both ends of the bridge. She and the bridge have a long history and she thinks of it in a unique way. "There's my friend," she says. "I think of that as I go to sleep at night and check it out when I wake up."

Don Pepper

WHEN DOES THE BRIDGE SWING?

"What time does the bridge swing over to Mackinac Island?" That question and others like it were asked of Dorothy Wallin many times in her years as a clerk at Teysen's Gift Shop. (By the way, the bridge does not swing.)

"My folks owned a restaurant (Lloyd's Café on Central Avenue) when I was a child," Dorothy said, "so I grew up with tourists around. I was quite used to them." As she got older, their questions were a source of amusement for her and her fellow workers at Teysen's, then later at the village offices where Dorothy spent over twenty years as village clerk. "You'd get off-the-wall questions that you tended to raise your eyebrows at," Dorothy recalled. "We'd get a smile and a laugh out of it after the people had gone. But then, I suppose if I went someplace strange, I'd ask a dumb question too.

Dorothy (Lloyd) Wallin

"One gentleman came in and was very upset," said Dorothy. "He said he could not understand why Michigan would build a bridge the size of the one here in this town. 'Why didn't they build it near a city where there would be something to do?' he asked. I said, 'Well, I imagine that the bridge is built over the Straits of Mackinac and this is where the Straits of Mackinac is located.' He just looked at me, turned around, and walked out."

Many downstaters didn't know what to expect when they arrived in relatively tiny Mackinaw City, and wondered what would await them after they crossed the bridge into the Upper Peninsula.

"We had people who would ask if they could buy postcards on the other side of the bridge," Dorothy said. "We'd tell them, 'Yes, you can even buy gum.' They thought there wouldn't be any stores when they got across the bridge--they'd just be in the wilderness. If they were buying something in the store here, they'd even ask if we could cash a five dollar bill.

"There was a standard joke about the bridge swinging over to the island once or twice a day," said Dorothy. "Some people wanted to take it to the island. They didn't want to go across to St. Ignace."

"My husband (Robert, now deceased) had a party come in one day at his office (at the car ferry dock at the south end of Mackinaw City). They were laughing because they were having the best time driving around town. They thought they were on Mackinac Island when they got to Mackinaw City. They were laughing because they knew there were supposed to be no cars driving around here. We ended up telling them exactly where they were. For a minute they thought they were right. Then they just went on out. I have no idea what these people thought all the other cars were doing here."

Dorothy's husband and children often joined Bridge Walkers on Labor Day. "He walked the first time and he didn't like to miss a year," Dorothy said of her husband. But she never accompanied her family. "I was busy making some money," she said. "Then later I worked (as a volunteer) selling tickets for the Bridge Walk. The people were all excited. It was kind of a family day. They were all good-natured and even after they'd stood in line for a couple of hours, they were still anxious to go. It's that last fling before school starts. There's quite a crowd—a lot of young children, people who go over in wheelchairs, people pulling kids in wagons--and it's all orderly. All those people in this little town and you never hear too much of anything going wrong. I think it's their big day out. You'll see them with their picnic baskets."

"There are a lot of people coming this way because of where my home is located (about four blocks from the bridge on Henry Street). You wake up in the morning and the cars are parked along all the streets. They've driven in around four or five o'clock in the morning to get a place to park. A lot of them walk past here because their cars are parked downtown and they're going back to their cars."

Dorothy enjoys sitting outside watching the Bridge Walkers. "I look at them and they're tired and hot and sweaty. I'll often ask, 'Did you have a good day?' They'll say 'Oh, it was great, but I'm so tired I don't think I'll make it to my car!' But they're back the next year to do the same thing over. They'll say, 'This is my tenth (or whatever) year.' They don't like to miss it. The kids all look like they've had a good time, and it's amazing the older people who walk the bridge."

After all these years of having the Mackinac Bridge as part of her life, Dorothy still likes to look at it. "I enjoy it. I really do. The novelty doesn't seem to wear off," she said with a smile.

John Wagner

Mackinaw City sits at the foot of the bridge.

ACKNOWLEDGEMENTS

Thank you to the many people who have made this book a reality:

Judy Bennett who taught me to use my computer and her digital camera.
John Childs who taught me to use his transcriber.
Ken Teysen whose photo graces the cover.
Ray Roth who was a spark plug for this project.
Cidney Roth who spent hours proofreading.
Sandy Planisek who edited and laid out the pages.
Countless others who have contributed photo and background information.
Tom Peters, my husband, who took me out to dinner when I simply didn't have the time or energy to cook after long hours of interviews or writing.
Members of the Mackinaw Area Historical Society who are dedicated to preservation of this area for future generations. And most of all, the many people whom I interviewed, whose love for the Mackinac Bridge is so contagious. They are the reason Mackinaw City is such a special place to live.

ABOUT THE AUTHOR

Mary Lou Peters and her husband Tom used to spend weekends in their cottage along the shores of the Straits of Mackinac. The more time they spent in the north country, the more they wanted to be there full-time. In 2004 they made their dream a reality and now call Mackinaw City their adoptive hometown.

Mary Lou is an active member of the Mackinaw Area Historical Society. As the 50th anniversary of the Mackinac Bridge approached she saw an opportunity, and felt a responsibility, to gather stories of some local residents who were impacted in many ways by the coming of the bridge.

The writing of this book was a labor of love—all proceeds from its sale go toward the development of the Mackinaw Area Historic Village.

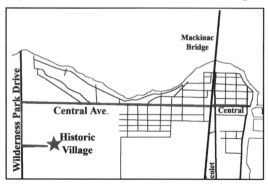